The ABC's of Nurturing Children

I0804077

26 Principles for Successful Parenting

The ABC's of Nurturing Children

Irene Kimmins

ISBN: 0-88290-362-4
Horizon Publishers' Catalog and Order Number: 2030
First Printing, April 1990

Printing: 1 2 3 4 5 6 7 8 9 10

Printed and distributed
in the United States of America by

Horizon Publishers
& Distributors, Incorporated
P.O. Box 490 Bountiful, Utah 84011-0490

How to Use This Book

The ABC's of Nurturing Children is laid out in two-page groups. In each group, the left page states the principle to be applied. The page on the right contains suggestions of pitfalls to be avoided in applying the principle.

After reading the book carefully, you may wish to devote a week to in-depth application of each principle, making it a habitual part of your parenting style. Memorize the principle. Express it often. Discuss it with other parents. Explore its ramifications. Make it *yours!* Apply it with love as you truly nurture your children.

Allow success.

Find tasks and activities that a child can do and gain a sense of accomplishment.

Avoid:

Giving advice: *"It'd be better if . . . ."*

Doing it for him: *"Here, let me because I can do it faster."*

Criticizing: *"You shouldn't leave wrinkles in your spread."*

Suggesting tasks or activities that are too difficult for his ability level.

Be proud of his efforts.

Accept a child's work and display it.
Give plenty of praise.

Avoid:

Comparing his work with someone else's: *"Johnny's painting looks more like a fire engine than yours."*

Correcting his work: *"Well, the grass should be green."*

Ignoring his work: *"Oh, that's nice, but I'm busy right now."*

Judging his work by your level of excellence: *"Kids draw such crazy things."*

Catch a child being good!

Tell him the behaviors that you like.

Avoid:

Nagging: *"sit still," "stand up straight," "slow down," "keep quiet!"*

Using constant negatives: *"no," "don't," "stop."*

Showing disapproval of every little thing: *"Not again. I've told you before not to do that."*

Making a child feel that you dislike him: *"You're so bad."*

Discuss feelings.

Learn to read your child's body language.
Allow him a chance to talk about his feelings and share your feelings with him.

Avoid:

Cutting off discussions: *"I don't have time now."*

Telling him how to feel: *"You can't be sad; it is only a dead cat."*

Denying a feeling: *"Big boys aren't afraid of the dark."*

Minimizing: *"Oh, you're not hurt. Stop making such a fuss."*

Establish schedules and routines.

Have regular times and routines to get up, go to bed, eat meals, take a bath, read a book, and other daily events so that your child feels secure in knowing what to expect.

Avoid:

Having no established way and time to do things.

Never changing routines or schedules so that there is no flexibility.

Sudden changes without warnings.

Friendly, but firm rules.

Explain rules and consequences at a calm time and in a calm manner. Follow through when needed.

Example:

State the consequence: *"I won't allow you to hit Jimmy."*

Present a choice: *"You can play the game without fighting or choose that I put it away."* (Fighting continues.)

Follow through: *"I see that you can not play without fighting."* (Put game away.)

Provide hope: *"Maybe next time you two can play without fighting."*

Avoid:

Physical punishment such as hitting, spanking and shaking.

Verbal abuse: "*You're so stupid.*"

Removing love: "*Mommy won't love you if you do that.*"

Threatening: "*If you do that again, you'll have to go to your room for the whole weekend.*"

Repeating, but not following through: "*That's the third time I've told you not to chase the cat.*"

Punishing when you're angry.

Give hugs, pats, and kisses.

Show affection and acceptance in appropriate, touching ways.

Avoid:

Assuming he knows of your love and affection: *"He knows I love him; I'm his father."*

Distance and indifference: *"Boys don't hug."*

Touching if your child does not want it: *"I'm just tickling him to make him laugh."*

Inappropriate sexual touching.

Help set goals.

Help your child make plans for something he wants to do by breaking the goal into smaller steps. Help him to see progress and encourage him to complete his goals.

Avoid:

Too long-range or too difficult goals.

Expectations of perfection.

Forcing your goals on him.

Never finishing anything.

Ignore attention-seeking (annoying) behaviors.

Give attention to behaviors you like or re-direct the child to another task.

Avoid:

Expecting a more grown-up behavior from a child.

Frustrating situations such as long waits, rushing or having to be still.

Debating over expected behavior at crisis points.

Rigid rules when a compromise may be in order.

Join with your child in laughter.

Be playful and find humor in life. Laughter is contagious.

Avoid:

Teasing and making fun of your child and his friends.

Public embarrassment.

Overburdening your child with familiy responsibilities and problems.

Always looking at what is wrong.

Know your child's rhythms.

Recognize his sleep patterns, energy level, appetite, attention span, coordination, temperament and maturity level.

Avoid:

Forcing your child to conform to someone else's rhythm.

Comparing his natural make-up with other children.

Overstimulating without helping him unwind.

Label behaviors, not kids.

Make clear that you like or dislike certain behaviors, but separate the behaviors from the child who uses them.

Avoid:

Name calling: *"'Fraidy Cat," "sissy," "fatty."*

Put downs: *"You're so clumsy," "you're careless," "you're selfish."*

Verbal abuse: *"You're really stupid. You can't do anything right."*

Letting others put labels on children. *"He's lazy." "She's a pig." "He's ugly."*

Make your child responsible for his actions.

Actions bring consequences. Allow your child to learn on his own by suffering consequences when needed.

Help him to think through his actions and see other possibilities.

Avoid:

Making choices for your child.

Telling your child what to do.

Removing consequences (unless dangerous to the child).

Expecting no mistakes.

Nudge a child to be curious and creative.

Encourage him to use his senses and to explore.

Provide the materials he needs for desired experiences.

Praise original ideas and accept unusual solutions.

Avoid:

Sterile environments.

Copying activities that have an improper standard.

Telling him what to do and how to do it.

Unlimited television viewing.

Organize the environment.

Try to see through your child's eyes. Make the surroundings appropriate to his needs and safety.

Teach your child to put away, to take care of, and to maintain his environment.

Avoid:

Disasters by preventing situations known to be harmful to children.

Unordered and chaotic surroundings.

Always cleaning up after a child.

Allowing a child to perform activities or make decisions that he is not mature enough to handle safely.

Play is a child's way to learn.

Let your child be a child. Allow him to discover life and to learn through play.

Avoid:

Unlimited television viewing.

Stressing only "educational" activities.

Organizing all of his time.

Putting him in competitive situations until he's skilled enough to handle them.

Quiet times need to be provided.

Let your child have time to daydream, to relax and to unwind.

Avoid:

Television as a quiet-time activity.

Constant noise and confusion.

Continual entertainment and activity.

Pressure to constantly accomplish or achieve.

Read to your child daily.

Make a habit of allocating time for reading and talking about books with him.

Avoid:

Your being too busy to read with or to your child.

Reading longer than the attention span of your child will allow.

Reading only educational material.

Watching television or videos in place of reading.

Share your values, traditions and religious beliefs.

Tell your child and show by example what you believe in and what you hold to be important.

Avoid:

Assuming that your child knows what you are thinking.

Saying one thing and doing another.

Expecting others to teach your child.

Demanding acceptance of your beliefs.

Talk with and listen to your child.

Take time to be with your child and use good communication skills such as eye contact, accepting feelings and using "I" statements.

Avoid:

Lecturing: *"It's wasteful to not . . . ."*

Explaining: *"Let me tell you how to do it right . . . ."*

Advising: *"You should . . . ."*

Correcting: *"You're doing it all wrong. Let me show you."*

Interrupting: *"What I have to say is more important."*

Ignoring: "I'm too busy now to . . . ."

Understand the way a child develops.

Learn the stages of growth that children go through so that you have reasonable expectations for your child.

Avoid:

Expecting a more mature behavior than your child is ready to display.

Pushing him to be more grown-up.

Being critical because you're embarrassed of his actions.

Letting others tell you what to do.

Value his uniqueness.

Help your child learn and experience life by using his senses. Respect his personal feelings and opinions.

Avoid:

Artificial learning experiences.

Telling your child what to think and feel.

Not permitting him to feel, touch, or smell objects.

Ridiculing his mistakes or wrong conclusions.

What your child can do for himself, let him.

Help him to learn independence and control of his environment.

Avoid:

Doing everything for your child.

Letting him make choices or decisions that are inappropriate for his age.

Removing responsibility for his choices and actions.

Not allowing challenges.

X

Expose your child to other cultures and experiences.

Help him to be understanding and appreciative of other people and their ways.

Avoid:

Making fun of others.

Criticizing others for being different.

Passing on prejudices and fears.

Promoting only one way of thinking.

You are the model.

Do as you want your child to do, for he will probably copy you.

Avoid:

Saying one thing and doing another.

Expecting perfection.

Setting higher standards for your child than for yourself.

Pressuring him to be what you would like him to be.

Zero in on safety and healthy habits.

Help your child recognize hazards and consequences.

Avoid:

Allowing your child to be in situations known to be harmful.

Allowing him to make decisions that he is not mature enough to make. You are the adult.

Permitting too many junk foods.

Promoting fear by being over-protective.

Discouraging physical activity.